W9-DFM-294

Outside and Inside
GIANT SQUID

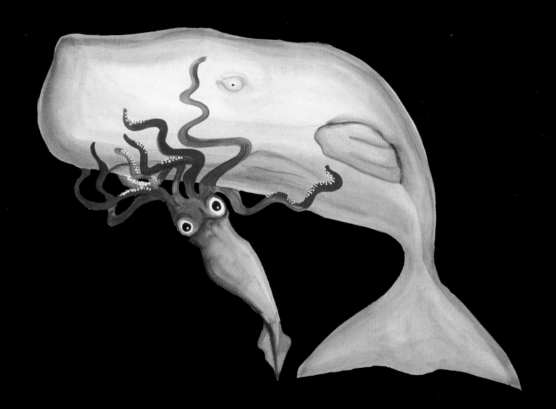

Sandra Markle

WALKER & COMPANY ❋ NEW YORK

For years, sailors told of seeing huge sea creatures that had long tentacles and big eyes. Everyone thought these stories were just tall tales. Then, in 1888, a 57-foot- (17-meter-) long squid washed ashore on a New Zealand beach. It was the biggest kind of squid anyone had ever seen. Scientists named the giant squid *Architeuthis dux* (ark-eh-TOOTH-is ducks), meaning ruling squid.

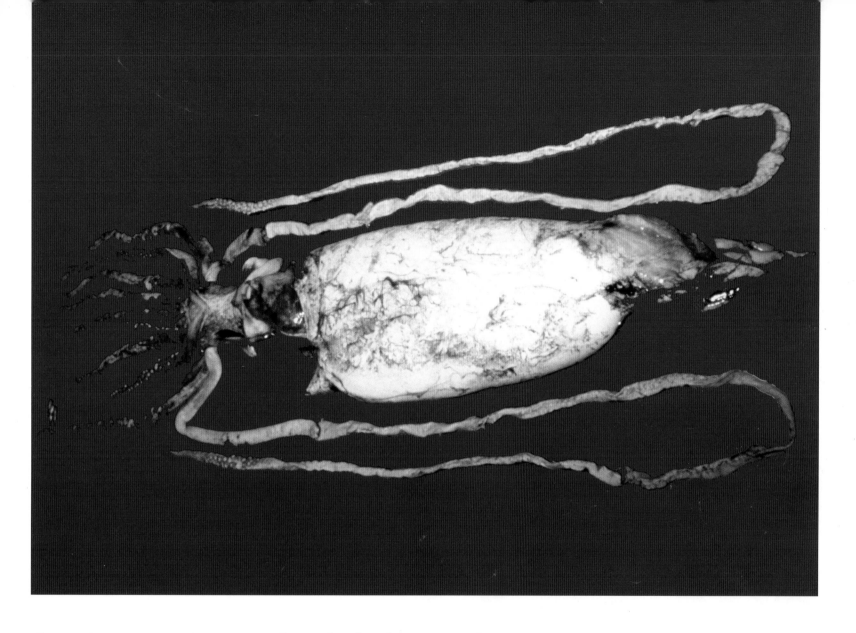

Over time, more giant squid washed ashore in other parts of the world. And still more were caught in fishing nets. Here you can see pieces of one that washed ashore. Seeing the dead bodies of *Architeuthis* made people wonder. What do giant squid eat? What are their lives like in the ocean? Could such giant creatures have any enemies? Turn the page to start investigating what has been discovered about these amazing ocean giants.

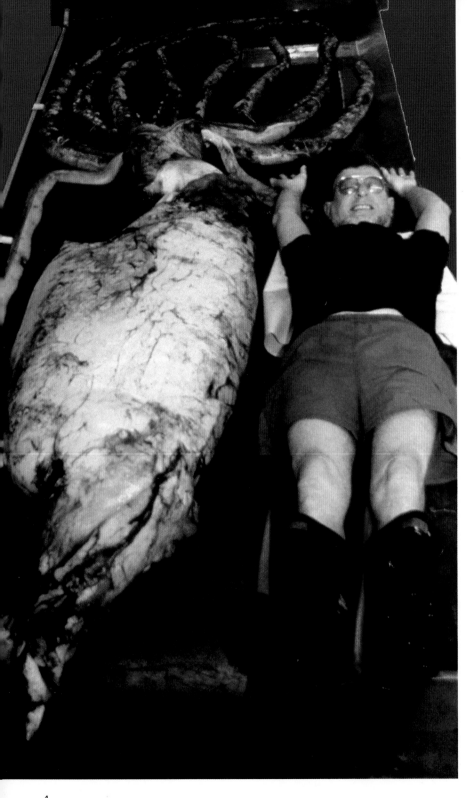

Giant squid expert Clyde Roper, who is six feet (1.8 meters) tall, is stretched out next to the body of an immature female *Architeuthis*. Clyde reported that had she lived to adulthood she might have nearly tripled her weight and grown at least fifteen feet (5 meters) longer—most of that length in tentacles.

After more than a century of searching, no one has ever—yet—been able to study a living giant squid. Scientists believe that's because *Architeuthis* lives in the deepest parts of the ocean. In 1997, Roper rode into the depths in a special submarine to search for one himself. But he didn't have any luck either. Still, Roper and others have learned a lot by studying dead giant squid. For one thing, unlike you, *Architeuthis* is an invertebrate. This means that giant squid lack a supporting skeleton of hard bones.

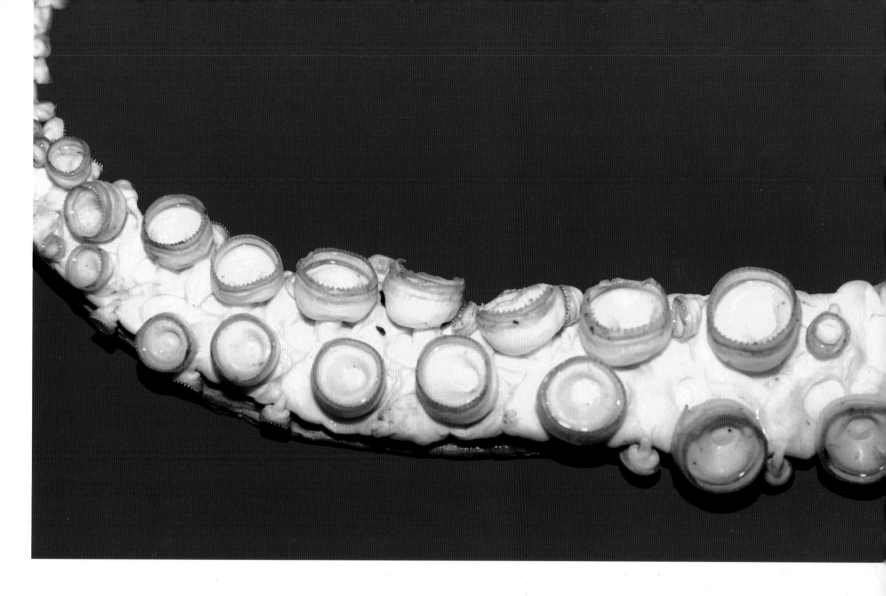

Here's just one of *Architeuthis*'s arms. A giant squid has eight arms and two longer tentacles. Stick out your tongue and wiggle it around to see how *Architeuthis*'s arms work. Like your tongue, the squid's arms are made up entirely of muscles, special body parts that work in pairs to pull against each other. But *Architeuthis*'s arms and tentacles are studded with suckers to lock onto prey. With these suckers, the giant squid can pull its prey to its mouth.

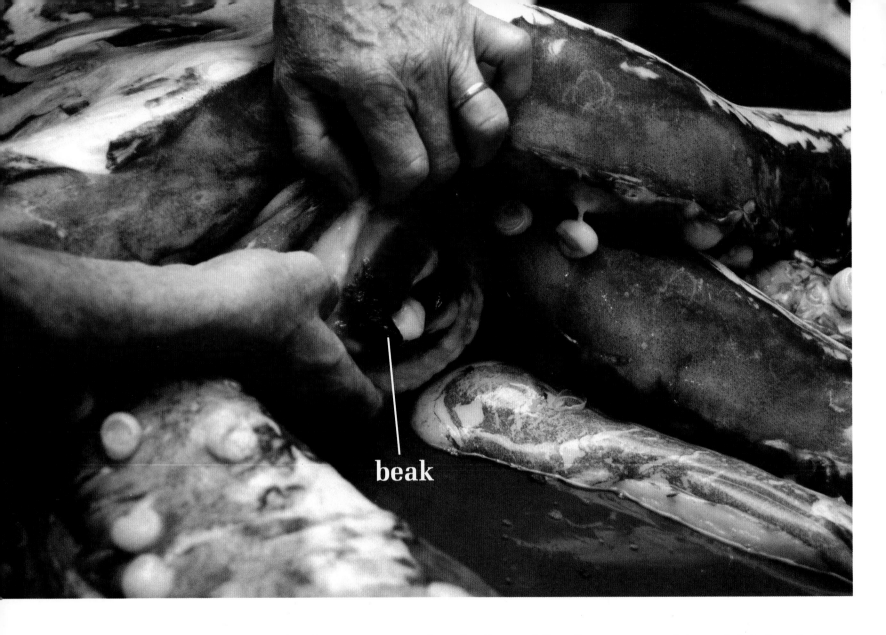

beak

Like all squid, *Architeuthis* has a strong, hook-shaped beak. But *Architeuthis*'s beak is as big as a man's hand.

By studying the giant squid's body parts, scientists have learned what these animals are capable of doing. From this information, they can make guesses about how giant squid live. Scientists also study other squid, like the jumbo squid shown here, that live in shallower water. All squid have certain features in common.

Most squid have torpedo-shaped bodies with eight arms and two tentacles.

An octopus may look a little like a squid at first glance, but its body has a rounder shape and lacks the two long tentacles.

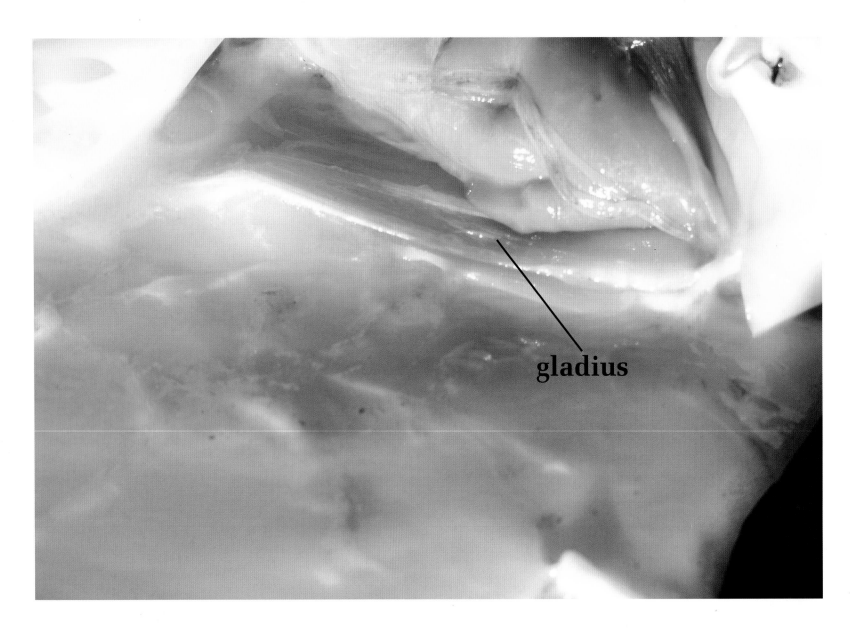

gladius

All squid have a body that's made up mostly of muscle. Here you can see the main supporting framework inside any squid. It's a central feather-shaped plate called the gladius.

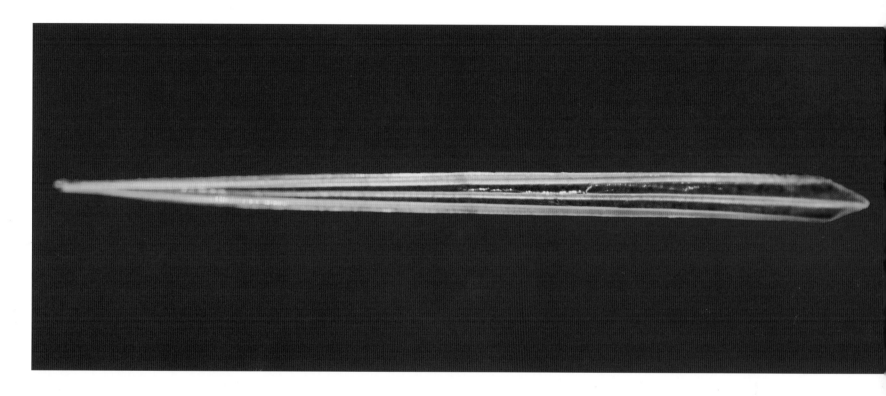

But the gladius isn't hard like bone. It's made of chitin, a material that is similar to your fingernails. To protect its brain and big eyes, a squid also has a helmetlike skull. Gently bend your ear and you can feel what a squid's skull is like. It's made of this same tough, bendable material called cartilage.

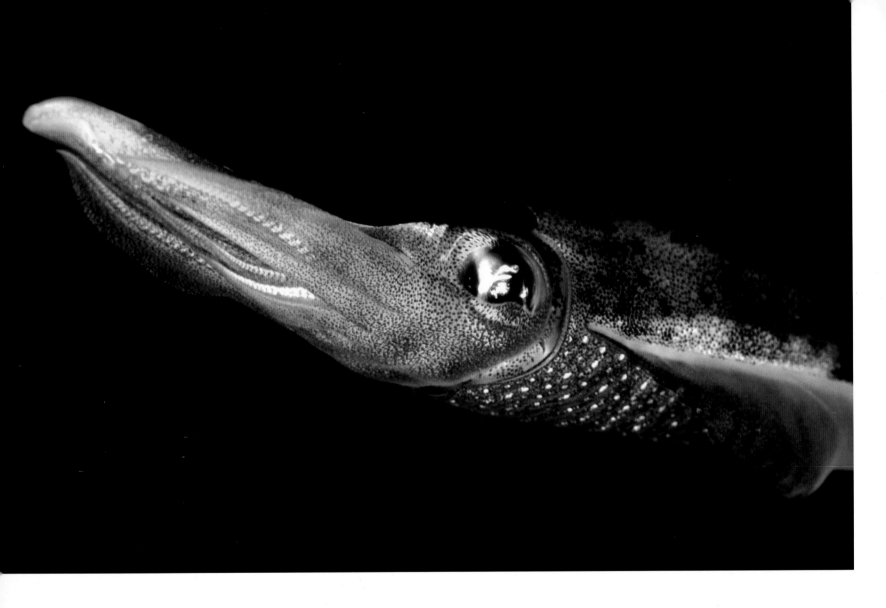

By watching squid, like this reef squid, scientists can see how *Architeuthis* moves in the deep sea. The outside of the squid's body is a tough muscular sac called the mantle. Like blowing up a balloon and letting the air escape, the squid draws water into its body and then squirts it out again.

Here you can see the funnel, the tube just below the squid's head where water squirts out. To start moving, the squid's brain sends signals to the muscles in the mantle wall. These signals travel through special pathways called nerves. When the muscles receive this signal, they relax. This action enables water to flow past the squid's head and into the mantle cavity. Next, the brain signals the muscles to contract. This movement closes the intake openings and pushes water out of the funnel. Because the funnel can be aimed in any direction, the squid can move forward, backward, up, down, and sideways.

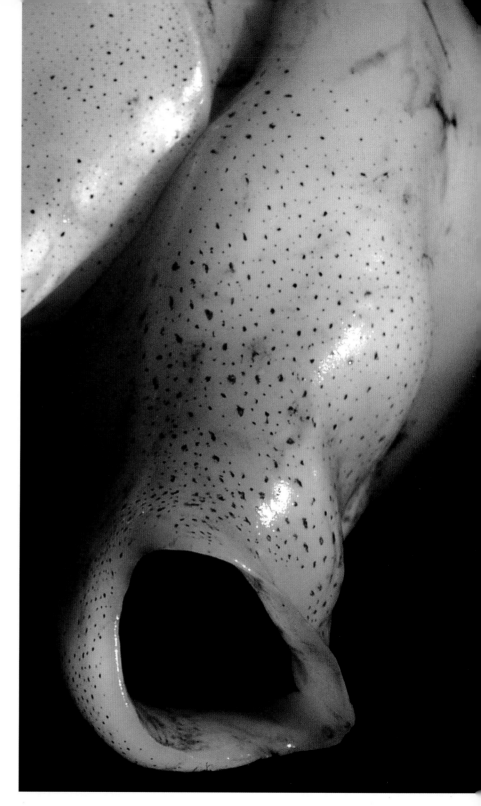

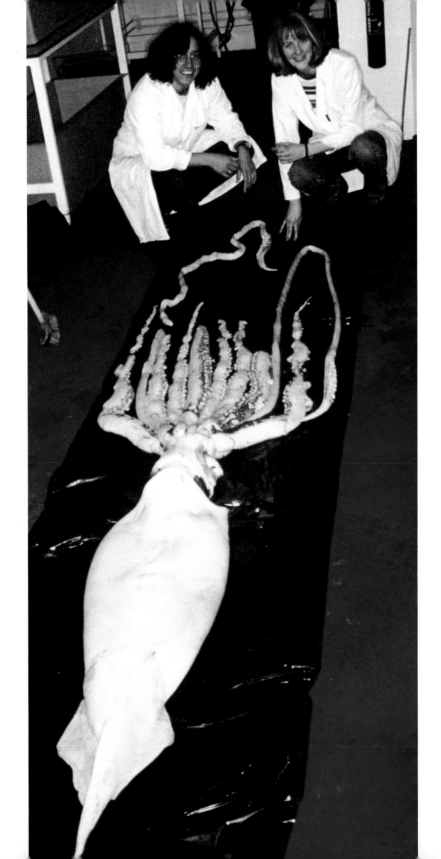

The heaviest *Architeuthis* ever found reportedly weighed 1,980 pounds (880 kilograms). But even that giant's body would be able to move easily in the sea. A giant squid tends to just naturally float. That's because its muscles contain ammonia, a chemical that's less dense than water. Look closely and you'll see two small fins on the giant squid's tail end. Like other squid, *Architeuthis* has fins to help it stay steady as it jets through the water.

Think about how much food a giant like *Architeuthis* must need to eat every day! Fish scales and bits of food found in *Architeuthis*'s stomach show that it mainly eats fish and smaller squid. First, though, it has to find its prey. That's where the giant squid puts its two long tentacles to work. These tentacles are as much as four to six times longer than *Architeuthis*'s body. They enable the giant squid to feel for prey. *Architeuthis* can even reach deep inside rocky crevasses.

Now, imagine being able to taste what you touch. A squid can do that. Its arms are studded with chemical sensors that send signals to its brain. So *Architeuthis* knows whether to grab onto something it touches or let it go.

Even though it can find food it can touch but not see, the main sense *Architeuthis* uses to hunt is sight. Like all squid, *Architeuthis* has big eyes so it can see well. In fact, a giant squid's eyes are the biggest in the ocean. They're as big as volleyballs! And each eye can move separately. So one eye may look up while the other looks down. Scientists believe such gigantic eyes may help *Architeuthis* detect deep-sea fish that glow. Giant squid may also be able to detect light waves that your eyes can't see.

Check out the fish this jumbo squid caught. Once a squid snags prey with its two long tentacles, it pulls the prey close enough to grab with some of its eight arms.

Look at these giant squid suckers. *Architeuthis* has suckers ranging in size from just a fraction of an inch (a few millimeters) across to about 2 inches (about 5 centimeters) across. And each arm and tentacle has about 300 suckers. Look closely and you'll see what helps them hold on—rings of sharp teeth!

Here you can see something else that helps *Architeuthis* handle its food. It's the tooth-studded strip called the radula, which is inside its mouth. First, the squid snips off a piece of food with its sharp beak. Then the radula locks onto the food and pushes it down the esophagus, the tube leading to the stomach. And, on the way to the stomach, the esophagus passes right through the squid's brain.

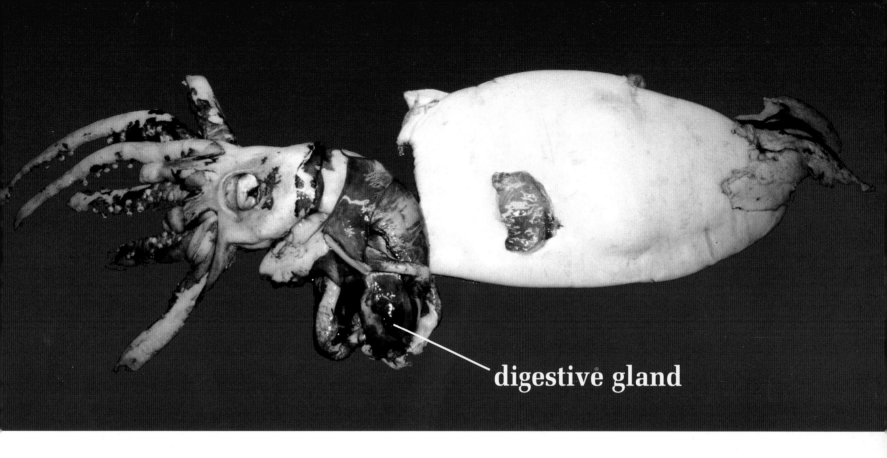

digestive gland

The squid's body parts are located inside its protective mantle. The food passes through the stomach and a large sac called the caecum. As the food moves, it's mixed with digestive juices produced by the digestive gland and turned into a paste. Then the paste is broken down into nutrients, the chemical building blocks of food. The nutrients pass through the walls of the caecum and into the blood. Any bits of food that didn't break down are ejected through the funnel into the water.

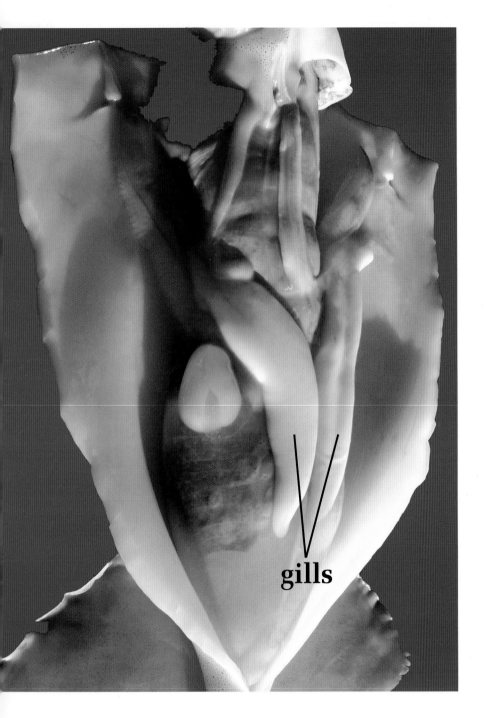

gills

Like all squid, *Architeuthis* needs more than food to live and be active. It also needs oxygen, a gas that's found in both air and water. As water is drawn into the squid's body, it passes through the gills. There water flows past spongy, feather-like parts. Then oxygen passes from the water into the blood. The blood also releases carbon dioxide, a waste gas, back into the water.

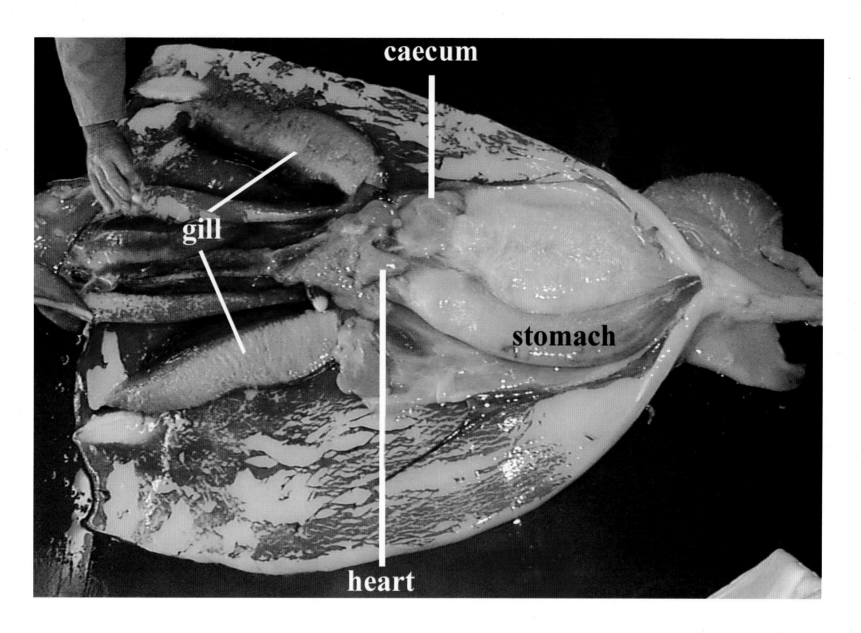

caecum

gill

stomach

heart

Take another peek inside *Architeuthis* to see what keeps a squid's blood moving. It's a special muscle—the heart. In fact, a squid has three hearts. The one you can see pumps blood through tubes to every part of the squid's body. Hidden beneath each gill is another heart to pump blood through the gill.

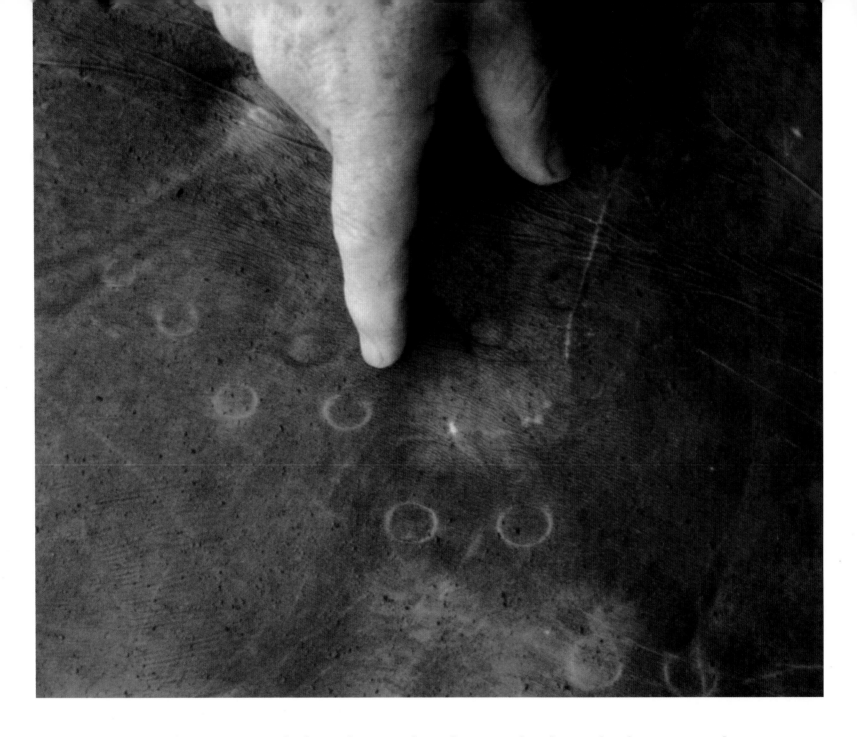

Check out this sperm whale's skin. What do you think made those round scars?

Did you guess that *Architeuthis*'s suckers scarred the whale? While a giant squid is growing up, it has lots of enemies, such as bigger fish, sharks, and even bigger squid. But once *Architeuthis* becomes a giant, it has just one main enemy—the sperm whale.

Sucker scars show *Architeuthis* fights back. But people who hunt whales have found lots of giant squid beaks in the stomachs of sperm whales. So it's likely the whales often win.

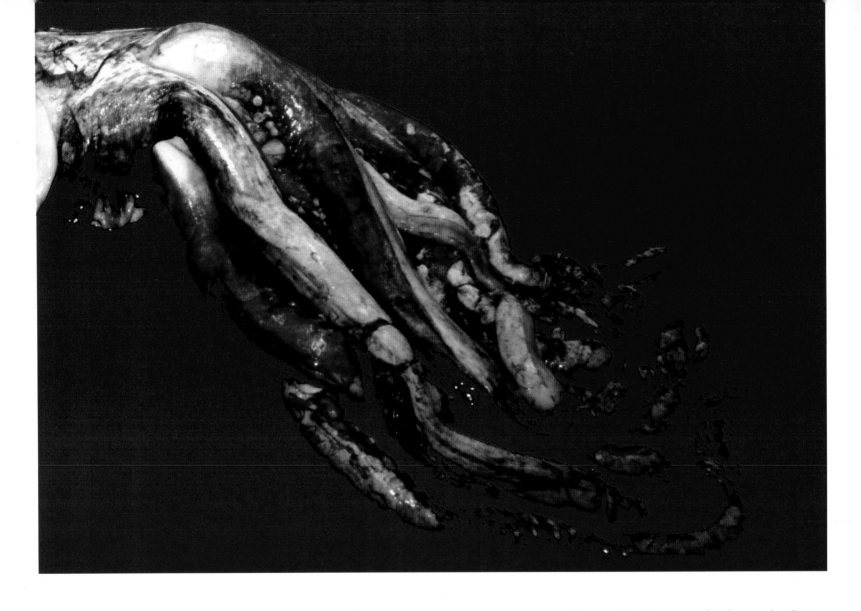

Look at the arms of this *Architeuthis*. You can see some of its dark purplish red skin. This coloring may help protect a giant squid from predators and is just right to let the squid hide in plain sight in the dark ocean depths. Dead giant squid only look white because this outer colored layer usually peels off after the squid dies.

Other kinds of squid have different ways to escape predators. This is a close-up view of a Caribbean reef squid's skin. What looks like colored dots are special cells called chromatophores, which contain yellow, orange, brown, red, or black coloring matter. Each chromatophore is like a plastic bag full of paint surrounded by a series of muscles. When the muscles relax, they push on the colored sac, keeping it small. When the muscles contract, they enable the chromatophore to expand into a big colored spot. Because much of the Carribbean reef squid's mantle is covered with chromatophores, it can change color almost instantly as it swims among colorful corals.

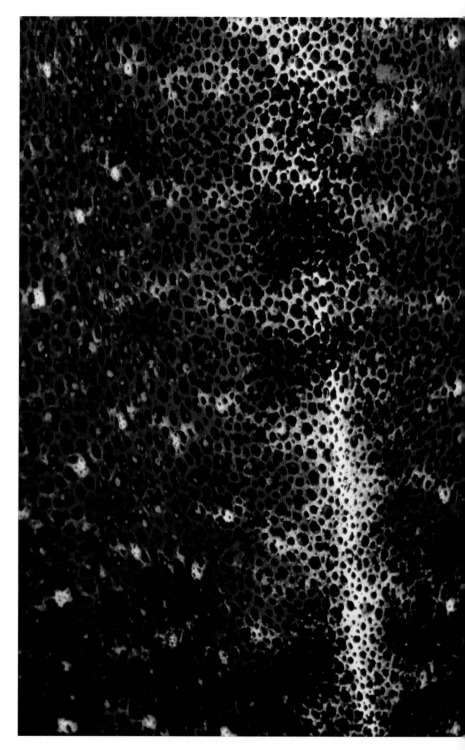

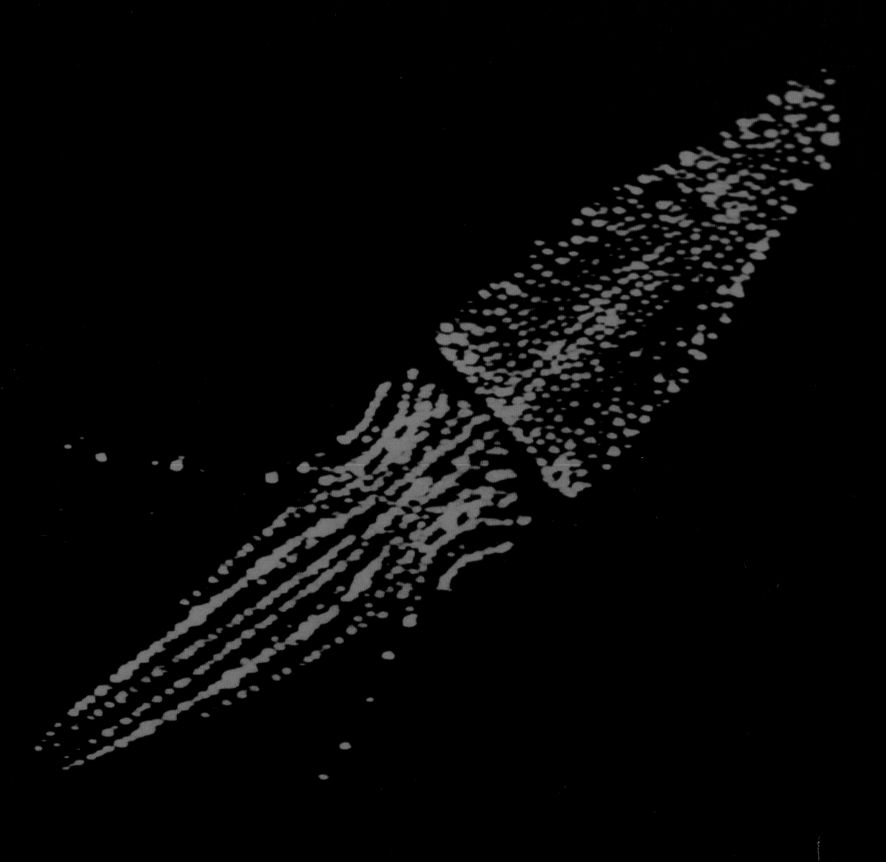

Still other squid have another trick to escape predators. They can light up. These squid have special cells called photophores, which produce light through a chemical reaction. If attacked, the squid flashes its lights suddenly. If it's lucky, this startles the predator long enough for the squid to escape.

And all squid have yet another escape trick. They shoot out a cloud of dark ink. This ink is produced and stored in a special ink sac at the end of the digestive system. Upon signals from the squid's brain, some or all of the ink is dumped into the body cavity. Then it's expelled with the next water blast. According to giant squid expert Clyde Roper, *Architeuthis* has an ink sac and may sometimes use this defense.

Besides eating and staying safe, the most important part of a squid's life is producing young. Scientists have yet to observe giant squid reproduction. But they guess the process is similar to that of other types of squid. Most squid show little interest in each other until it's time to mate. Then, some, like market squid, swarm together by the millions.

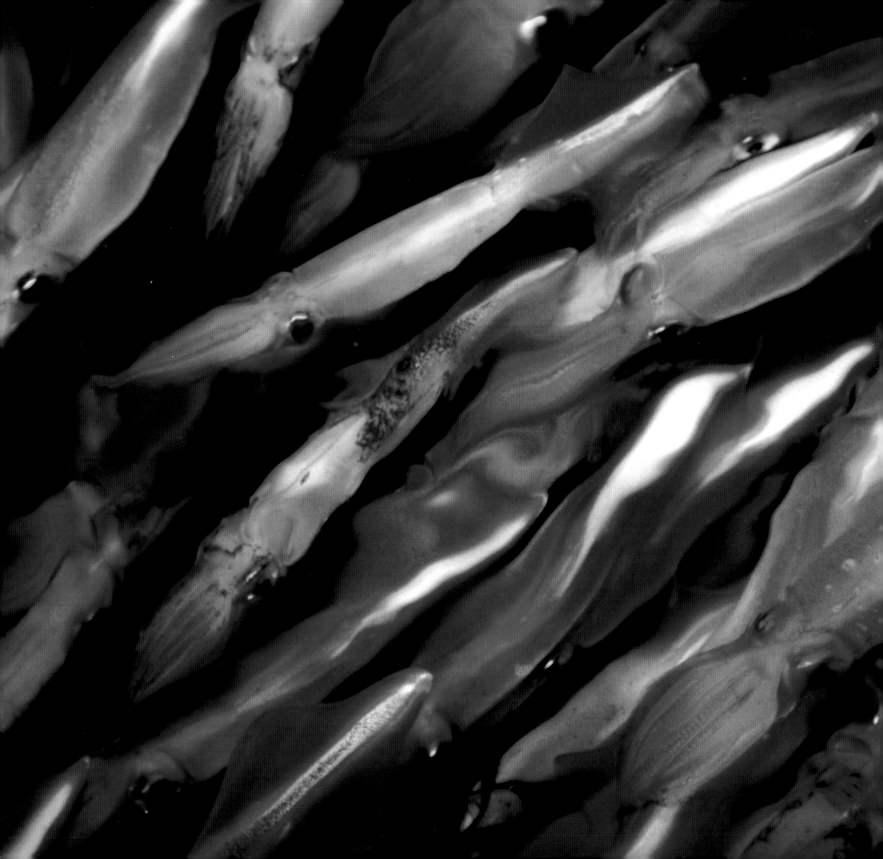

This market squid pair hovers over masses of eggs laid by other market squid.

The males produce gelatinlike packets of special reproductive cells, called sperm. When the squid mate, the males transfer these packets to the female. Then, inside the mantle cavity, the sperm join with the female's reproductive cells, called eggs.

Scientists have found as many as 10 million eggs inside a female *Architeuthis.* Each of these was less than an inch (about 2 millimeters) long. No one knows if the giant squid female deposits her eggs in a mass, like the market squid, or if she releases her eggs one by one into the sea. Clyde Roper reports that scientists can only guess what happens next. For most kinds of squid, reproduction is the natural end of their life cycle. So scientists believe that *Architeuthis* parents probably die shortly after reproducing. Because the eggs develop unguarded, predators, such as sharks, may eat some of the eggs.

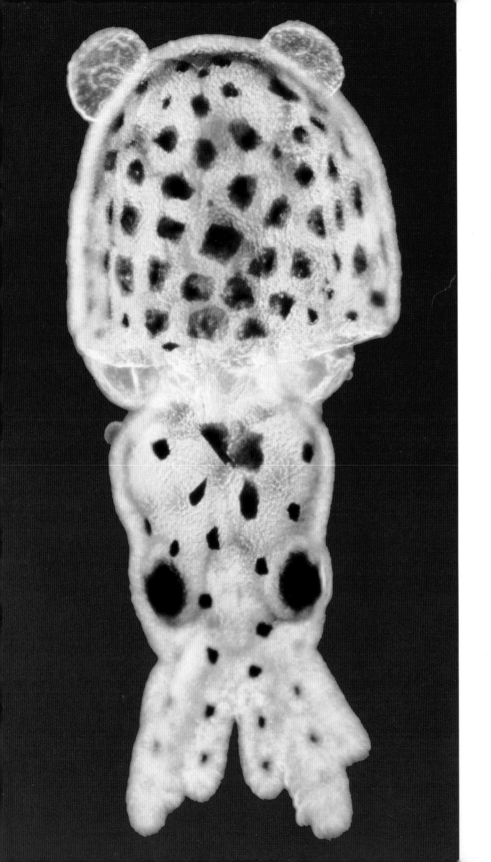

This is a newly hatched market squid. The length of time it takes for any young squid to hatch depends on the water temperature—the colder the water, the longer it takes. But once the squid hatches, it's on its own to stay safe while it grows up. So how long does it take a young *Architeuthis* to become a giant?

This bone found inside a giant squid's head could help scientists find out. Squid expert Martin Collins discovered that other types of squid have this bone too. And in those squid, the bone becomes one ring bigger every day. Of course, scientists will only know for sure how fast *Architeuthis* grows when they can study living giant squid.

And there are still many other mysteries to be solved. For example, what does a young *Architeuthis* eat? And how does it escape being eaten? Maybe, one day, you'll be the one to observe *Architeuthis* alive in the ocean depths. Then you'll discover the rest of the giant squid's secrets!

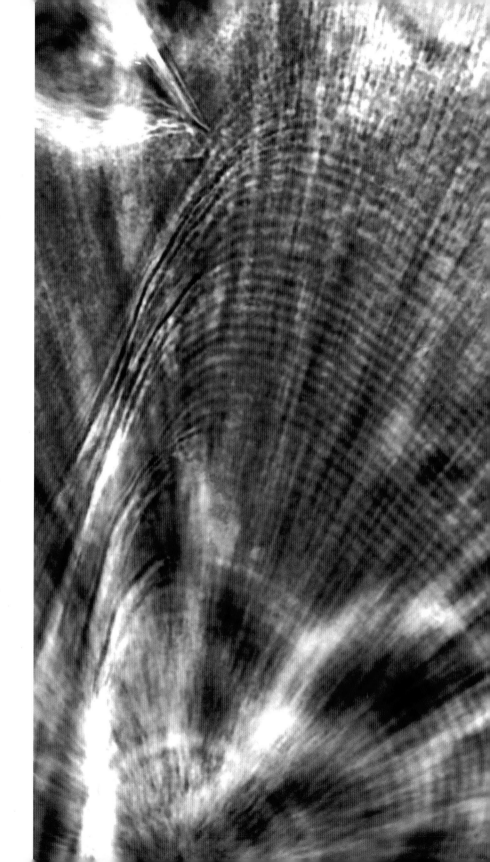

Glossary/Index

Words that appear in red in the text are included in the glossary.
A special pronunciation guide has been added with each entry to help readers sound out the words.

AMMONIA   *uh-MOAN-yuh*   A chemical less dense than water that is stored in spaces among muscle fibers in *Architeuthis* and other squid. **15**

ARM   *aarm*   A long, muscular body part attached to the head. Each arm has two rows of suckers that enable a squid to pull prey into its mouth, which is located at the center of its ring of eight arms. **5, 8, 16, 20**

BEAK   *beek*   The hard, sharp projecting part of a squid's mouth. Its shape is similar to a parrot's beak. **6, 22, 27**

BLOOD   *blud*   The fluid that flows through a squid's body, carrying food and oxygen to all body parts and flushing away wastes. **24–25**

BRAIN   *brayn*   The central body part that receives and analyzes messages about what is happening inside and outside the body. The brain sends instructions to put the body into action. **11, 13, 16, 22, 31**

CAECUM   *SEE-kum*   A body part in which special digestive juices finish breaking down food into nutrients. **23**

CARBON DIOXIDE   *KAR-bun die-OXS-eyed*   A waste gas that is naturally released during various bodily functions. It is carried to the gills by the blood and released into the water that is expelled from the body through the funnel. **24**

CHROMATOPHORE   *kroh-MAT-oh-for*   A pigment-containing organ that expands or contracts, causing the squid's skin to change color. **29**

DIGESTION   *die-JEST-chen*   The process whereby chemicals break down food. **22–24, 31**

EGG   *eg*   The name given to the female reproductive cell. It is also the name given to the fertilized egg that will produce a baby squid. **34–35**

ESOPHAGUS   *eh-SOF-fah-gus*   A tube leading to the squid's stomach. **22**

EYE   *ii*   The body part that lets the squid see. When light enters the eye, messages are sent to the brain, where they are analyzed. **11, 18–19**

FIN   *fin*   The body part that helps a squid travel in a steady, straight path as it jets through the water. **14–15**

FUNNEL   *FUNN-l*   The body part that sticks out of the mantle opening just below the head. Water jets out the funnel to expel wastes and ink and to propel the squid through the water. The female also deposits eggs through her funnel. **13, 23**

GILL — *gil* The body part in which oxygen and carbon dioxide gas are exchanged. **24–25**

GLADIUS — *GLADE-ee-us* A tough and flexible feather-shaped blade that provides internal support for the squid's organs and attachment for some of its muscles. **11**

HEART — *haart* The body part that acts like a pump, constantly circulating blood. A squid has three hearts. The main heart pumps blood throughout its entire body. Each gill also has a heart to pump blood from each gill to the main heart. **25**

INK — *ingk* A dark liquid produced and stored by a special body part and ejected through the funnel in an effort to confuse predators. **31**

MANTLE — *MANT-l* A muscular body part that envelops the internal organs of the squid. **12–13, 23, 29, 35**

MUSCLE — *MUHS-l* A body part that produces movement. Muscles usually work in pairs. **5, 11–15, 29**

NERVES — *nurvz* Pathways that connect all parts of the squid's body to its brain. **13**

NUTRIENTS — *NOO-tree-ntz* Chemical building blocks into which food is broken down for use by the squid's body. **23**

OCTOPUS — *AHK-tu-puss* A sea animal that is related to squid and has a soft, oval-shaped body and eight arms studded with suckers. **9**

OXYGEN — *AHKS-y-jen* A gas in the water that passes into the squid's blood in the gills. The blood then carries it through the body, where it is combined with food nutrients to release energy. **24**

PHOTOPHORE — *FOH-tuh-for* A light-producing body part. **30–31**

PREDATOR — *PRED-uh-tor* An animal that catches and eats other animals. **29, 31**

PREY — *pray* The food that an animal catches and eats. **5, 16, 20–21**

RADULA — *RADJ-uh-luh* The body part in a squid's mouth studded with teeth. It pushes food into the esophagus, a tube leading to the squid's stomach. **22**

REPRODUCTION — *ree-pruh-DUCK-shun* The process through which male and female squid produce offspring. **32–36**

SPERM — *spurm* The male reproductive cell. When the sperm joins with the female's egg, a baby squid develops. **35**

SPERM WHALE — *spurm wayl* The largest of the toothed whales. It is the main predator of adult giant squid. **26–27**

STOMACH — *STUM-mek* Body part in which special juices begin to break down food. **16, 22–23**

SUCKER — *SUK-r* A cup-shaped structure on a squid's tentacles and arms used to hold onto prey. **5, 20–21, 27**

TENTACLE — *TENT-uh-kl* A long, flexible body part near the squid's head used to grasp and hold onto prey. **5, 8–9, 16, 20**

With love, for Katrina and Andrew Chase

First published in the United States of America in 2003 by
Walker Publishing Company, Inc.

Published simultaneously in Canada by Fitzhenry and Whiteside, Markham, Ontario L3R 4T8

For information about permission to reproduce selections from
this book, write to Permissions, Walker & Company, 435 Hudson Street, New York, New York 10014

Library of Congress Cataloging-in-Publication Data

Markle, Sandra.
Outside and inside giant squid / Sandra Markle.
p. cm.
Summary: Describes the inner and outer workings of giant squids, enormous deep-sea creatures that have never been seen alive, discussing their diet, anatomy, and reproduction.
ISBN 0-8027-8872-6 — ISBN 0-8027-8873-4 (rein)
1. Giant squids—Juvenile literature. [1. Giant squids. 2. Squids.] I. Title.

QL430.3.A73 M37 2003
594'.58—dc21
2002191044

Book design by Victoria Allen

Visit Walker & Company's Web site at www.walkerbooks.com

Printed in Hong Kong

2 4 6 8 10 9 7 5 3

Acknowledgments: The author would like to especially thank Dr. Clyde Roper, Department of Invertebrate Zoology, National Museum of Natural History, Smithsonian Institution, Washington, D.C., U.S.A., for sharing his research, his time, and his enthusiasm for studying *Architeuthis*. The author would also like to thank the following people for sharing their expertise: Martin Collins, British Antarctic Survey, Cambridge, England; Dr. George Jackson, University of Tasmania, Hobart, Tasmania; and Professor Chung Cheng Lu, Department of Zoology, National Chung Hsing University, Taichung, Taiwan. Finally, a special thanks to Skip Jeffery, who shared the effort and joy of creating this book.

Note to Parents and Teachers: The books in the Outside and Inside series enable young readers to discover how different animals are uniquely suited to survive. Kids investigate the physical features and behaviors that cause these animals to be successful in their particular environment.

Photo Credits

Cover: courtesy Sandra Markle
Page 1: courtesy Sandra Markle
Page 2: courtesy Sandra Markle
Page 3: courtesy Clyde Roper
Page 4: courtesy I. H. Roper
Page 5: courtesy Sandra Markle
Page 6: courtesy Clyde Roper
Page 7: courtesy Mark Conlin/Innerspace
Page 8: courtesy G. Williamson/Bruce Coleman
Page 9: courtesy Ed Egginger/Bruce Coleman
Page 10: courtesy Skip Jeffery

Page 11: courtesy Skip Jeffery
Page 12: courtesy Marc Bernardi/Innerspace
Page 13: courtesy Skip Jeffery
Page 14: courtesy Martin Collins
Page 17: courtesy Clyde Roper
Page 18: courtesy Bob Cranston/Innerspace
Page 20: courtesy Bob Cranston/Innerspace
Page 21: courtesy Sandra Markle
Page 22: courtesy C. C. Lu
Page 23: courtesy Clyde Roper
Page 24: courtesy Skip Jeffery

Page 25: courtesy C. C. Lu
Page 26: courtesy Clyde Roper
Page 28: courtesy Clyde Roper
Page 29: courtesy Doug Perrine/Innerspace
Page 30: courtesy Elizabeth Widder
Page 33: courtesy Lewis Trusty/Animals Animals
Page 34: courtesy Mark Conlin/Innerspace
Page 36: courtesy George Jackson
Page 37: courtesy Martin Collins